The Little Chick

Copyright @2021 by NAT WILLIAMS

All rights reserved. No part of this book may be reproduced in any form or by any electronic or mechanical means, including information storage and retrieval systems, without permission in writing from the publisher, except by reviewers, who may quote brief passages in a review.

This publication contains the opinions and ideas of its author. It is intended to provide helpful and informative material on the subjects addressed in the publication. The author and publisher specifically disclaim all responsibility for any liability, loss or risk, personal or otherwise, which is incurred as a consequence, directly or indirectly, of the use and application of any of the contents of this book.

WORKBOOK PRESS LLC
187 E Warm Springs Rd,
Suite B285, Las Vegas, NV 89119, USA

Website: https://workbookpress.com/
Hotline: 1-888-818-4856
Email: admin@workbookpress.com

Ordering Information:
Quantity sales. Special discounts are available on quantity purchases by corporations, associations, and others. For details, contact the publisher at the address above.

ISBN-13: 000-0-00000-000-0 (Paperback Version)

000-0-00000-000-0 (Digital Version)

REV. DATE:

The Little Chick

WRITTEN BY:

NAT WILLIAMS

There once was a little chick
Who had just broken out of her
Shell and decided to take a walk.

"What a long and ugly nose you have," Said the little chick to the elephant. "I'm glad I don't have a nose like that!"

"That's not very nice," said the elephant. "One day you might wish you had a long nose."

"Not me," said the little chick softly to herself.

"What long big ears you have," said the little chick to the rabbit. "I'm glad I don't have big ears."

"But I hear very well with my ears. No one could ever sneak up on me."

"Who cares," said the little chick.

"Well," said the rabbit as he climbed into his hole, "one day you might wish you had long ears."

"Note me!" said the little chick as she walked along.

"I'm glad I don't have big teeth like yours," said the little chick to the beaver.

"That's not a very nice thing to say. My teeth are very useful. One day you might wish you had sharp teeth like mine."

"Not me," said the little chick.

"What a long skinny legs you have," said the little chick to the ostrich. "You look like a king-sized turkey."

"I'm one of the fastest animals in the world," said the ostrich.

"Who cares," said the little chick.

"Well," said the ostrich, "one day you might wish you had long legs."

"Not me," said the little chick.

Finally, the little chick met a fox who was having lunch.

"Would you like to join me for lunch?" asked the sly fox, smacking his lips.

"Sure!" said the little chick. The fox quickly grabbed the little chick and tied her to a tree. "Oh my!" cried the little chick.

"Oh how I wish I had a sharp teeth like the beaver so I could cut these ropes, or long fast legs like the ostrich."

"The little chick needs help," said the rabbit as he hid behind the hill.

And he hopped back to get help from the other animals. "The little chick needs help," said the rabbit.

"I'll cut the ropes," said the beaver.

"I'll carry her back home," said the ostrich. So Before the fox knew what happened, the beaver had cut the ropes, and the ostrich raced back home, with the little chick on his back.

"Thank you very much," said the little chick. "If only I had long legs or sharp teeth."

"Not everyone can be fast or have sharp teeth," said the ostrich.

"We have to do the best with what we have," said the beaver.

"And never make fun of someone just because they look different," said the rabbit.

"I never will again," said the little chick.

THE END

About The Author

Nat Williams is an elementary teacher in the Pittsburgh Public School District. He has been teaching children for over thirty years. Nat's love for children began in high school, where he coached seven-to-eight-year-old baseball players. During the summer months in college, Nat taught archery at a camp in Maine. Upon graduating college, Nat taught archery at a camp in Maine. Upon graduating college, Nat did substitute teaching along with coaching girl's gymnastics. He eventually landed full-time employment with the Pittsburgh Public Schools. Nat has ended his coaching career, and has decided to concentrate on writing children's books. He hopes that children will not only enjoy this book, but also learn from it.

www.ingramcontent.com/pod-product-compliance
Lightning Source LLC
Chambersburg PA
CBHW061106070526
44579CB00011B/155